Art & Activities for Kids

Make Costumes!

FOR CREATIVE PLAY

Priscilla Hershberger

NORTH LIGHT BOOKS

Cincinnati, Ohio

A Word About Safety

The activities in this book were developed for the enjoyment of children. We've taken every precaution to ensure their safety and success. Please follow the directions, and note where an adult's help is required. In fact, feel free to work alongside your young artists as often as you can. They will appreciate help in reading and learning new techniques, and will love the chance to talk and show off their creations. Children thrive on attention and praise, and craft adventures are the perfect setting for both.

This hardcover edition of *Make Costumes!* features a "self-jacket" that eliminates the need for a separate dust jacket. It provides sturdy protection for your book while it saves paper, trees and energy.

96 95 94 93 92   5 4 3 2 1

Library of Congress Cataloging in Publication Data

Hershberger, Priscilla Gorman.
    Make costumes! : for creative play / Priscilla Gorman Hershberger.—1st ed.
        p.   cm.—(Art & activities for kids)
    Summary: Presents step-by-step instructions for making a variety of garments using easy-to-find supplies.
    ISBN 0-89134-450-0
    1. Costume—Juvenile literature. 2. Handicraft—Juvenile literature.
[1. Costume. 2. Handicraft.] I. Title. II. Series.
TT633.H45   1992
616.4'78—dc20
                                                    92-2817
                                                    CIP
                                                    AC

Edited by Julie Wesling Whaley
Design Direction by Clare Finney
Art Direction by Kristi Kane Cullen
Photography by Pamela Monfort
Very special thanks to Donna Conrady-Miller, Marilyn Daiker, Leanne Greensberg, Kevin Houillion, Jennifer Mayhall, Kathy Savage-Hubbard, Judith Turner, Mary Wesling, and Suzanne Whitaker.

About This Book (A Note to Grown-Ups)

Make Costumes! features twenty-five unique and diverse projects for making costume pieces. You might think costumes are only for Halloween. But that's just the beginning! These costume ideas are so easy and so much fun, your kids will want to use the book to dress up for creative play throughout the year. Twenty-one complete costumes are showcased to fire the imaginations of girls and boys ages six to eleven.

In *Make Costumes!*, kids learn how to make tops, knickers, capes, hats, accessories, hair, even shoes. The projects provide clear step-by-step instructions and photographs. But they're open-ended, allowing for limitless creative expression as kids decide how to combine garments to create any costume they imagine. In this way, kids exercise problem-solving skills in addition to artistic skills. Wait until you see the look on a child's face when he learns *he* can *make* something to wear—without sewing—out of scrap cloth, old towels or sheets or a tablecloth, or even a shower curtain or paper shopping bag! With a little imagination, a swatch from a discarded throw rug can become fake fur trim.

Getting the Most Out of the Projects

These projects are fun for parents and kids to do together, and simple enough for kids to do on their own. Best of all, young "costume designers" will beam when someone admires a garment they've made themselves, something not possible with store-bought costumes or outfits adults make for them.

Costuming provides a wonderful opportunity for self-expression. Kids can dress up in a way that they don't normally. They can imitate legendary characters or create new ones. They can use costumes for make-believe, or for acting out favorite storybooks or movies or nursery rhymes. You might want to discuss with your child how to put on a staged play: how to write the story, make a simple set, and decide who will do and say what.

Most of the garments in this book are easy to make in a short amount of time. Others require more patience and even adult supervision. The adult and child symbol explained on page 6 will help you recognize the more challenging activities.

The list of materials shown at the beginning of each activity indicates what was used to make the featured project. Suggested alternatives may require different supplies. Feel free to substitute! Almost anything can be turned into a costume. The projects are totally flexible to make it easy for you and your child to make as many costumes as you wish.

Collecting Supplies

All of the projects can be done with household items or inexpensive, easy-to-find supplies. (See page 7 for definitions of any craft materials you're not already familiar with.) Here are some household items you'll want to make sure you have on hand: scrap cloth or old sheets, pillowcases, tablecloths, curtains, towels, etc.; thin cardboard such as poster board and empty cereal boxes; white glue; masking tape; any old clothes, including pants, skirts, nylon stockings, and socks; paper bags—shopping bags, grocery bags, and lunch bags; aluminum foil; string and rope; plastic lids from milk or juice bottles; needle and thread; yarn; safety pins.

28
Hair
Make straight, braided, or long, curly hair for your costume. It's easy when you use yarn, nylon stockings, or rope. See how to make *really* long hair for a Rapunzel costume!

32
Shoes
Decorate your own shoes or ballet slippers, or make moccasins out of felt or fabric. Make boots out of cloth or paper. Lunch bags become big shoes. Turn socks into three-toed feet for birds and animals.

42
Hats
Make a cone-shaped hat for a princess, witch, wizard, or clown. Make a cap with or without a brim. Or cut out a paper hat for Robin Hood. All you need to get started is paper and tape.

46
Accessories
A queen's costume wouldn't be complete without a crown and a scepter. Can you imagine a bee without wings? Learn how to put the finishing touches on these and other costumes. Make safe weapons for a pirate or Robin Hood.

Finished Costumes
Throughout this book, you will find kids wearing finished costumes. You don't have to copy them exactly! We hope the pictures will give you ideas you can use to create your own costumes.

Be a Good Artist

Work Habits

Get permission to set up a costume workshop. If you use glue or paint, cover your workspace with newspapers or a vinyl tablecloth.

Don't waste clothes or good cloth! Plan before you begin. Draw your designs on paper to experiment. Try your ideas on scrap cloth.

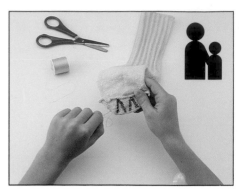

Follow the directions carefully for each project. When you see the adult and child symbol, have an adult help you.

Don't put art materials in your mouth. If you're working with a younger child, don't let him put art materials in his mouth, either.

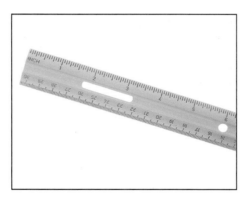

Use a ruler to measure. This symbol, ″, means inches (12″ means twelve inches). Cm means centimeters. (About 2½ cm equals 1″.)

Always finish each project by cleaning your workshop. Have fun, but be careful and treat all your tools with respect.

How to Sew

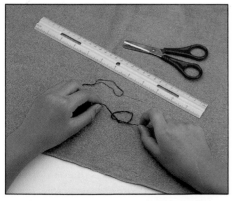

1 Cut a long piece of thread and poke it through the eye (hole) of a needle. Pull the ends even and tie a knot.

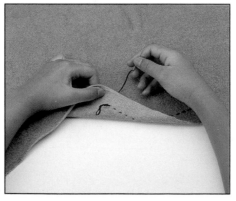

2 Sew with small stitches in and out of your fabric. Check each stitch to be sure your thread hasn't tangled underneath.

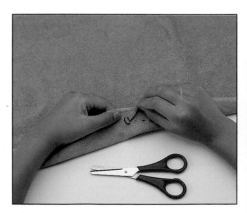

3 After you've stitched awhile, the thread will get short. Push the needle to the back of your work, make a knot, and cut the thread.

Craft Materials

Almost any of the costumes in this book can be made out of paper instead of cloth. Paper is easy to use, but costumes made out of paper may not last as long as costumes made out of cloth. Costumes made out of paper should not be worn outside on a rainy day!

If you know how to sew, or know an adult who can help you, then you should sew cloth costume pieces together because it is the strongest way. If you don't want to sew, you can put costumes together with tape or glue. Taping or gluing will be faster, but your costumes may not last as long. You should decide whether your costume will be for one day of play or something you will want to keep for a long time.

Masking tape is strong enough to hold cardboard or fabric. Wide masking tape holds better than thin masking tape. *Duct tape* is even stronger, but it is harder to use because it's so sticky. You can buy either kind of tape at a supermarket or hardware store.

Fabric glue is a special kind of white glue you can buy at fabric stores or craft stores. Look for a label that says "permanent" or "washable." Then you'll know it won't wash out after it's dry. Use it to glue fabric pieces together, and to attach ribbon, lace, sequins, and glitter.

Thread. Regular sewing thread is strong enough for all the projects in this book. If you want the stitches to show (see Robin Hood's top on page 12 and boots on page 34), then you can use a big needle and sew with yarn.

Paint. You can use several kinds of paint on your costumes: fabric paint (shown here in red), tempera paint (orange), and acrylic paint (blue).

Fabric paint is specially made for cloth. There are many kinds of fabric paint, including glitter paint and puffy paint. You can buy fabric paint at fabric stores and craft stores. Always follow the directions on the fabric paint label.

Tempera paint, also called poster paint, is a water-based paint that is opaque—you can't see through it. You can buy it in art supply stores, craft stores, and some supermarkets. It is fine for paper. Use it on cloth *only* if you don't intend to wash your costume, because tempera paint can wash out of cloth.

Acrylic paint is a water-based plastic paint that's thick and shiny. It comes in a tube or squeeze bottle. You can buy it at art supply stores and craft stores. You mix it with water to paint. It won't wash out of most cloth, but you should test it on a little piece before you paint your whole costume.

Scissors. Scissors need to be sharp to cut through fabric. Be careful when you cut with them. Test different scissors in your house until you find a pair that will cut cloth easily. If you buy a new pair just for fabric, mark them "sewing" and don't use them for paper. That way, they'll stay sharp longer.

Pinking shears are special scissors that cut a zigzag line. Cutting with them will help keep the cut edge from *fraying.* Fraying is when the threads pull off, making the cut edge look rough and unfinished. Look carefully at the devil's cape and boots on pages 30 and 33. They were cut with pinking shears.

7

Tops

Tops are super simple to make. You can make beautiful long tops for costumes like witches, wizards, angels and movie stars. Or make a short top for a monster, pirate, ballerina or clown. The first step is always to fold the cloth in half so that your top will have a front and a back. Then you can hold it up against your body, with the fold under your chin, to see how long it will be. It's fun to cut shapes in the cloth or add sleeves. You can even make short tops out of paper shopping bags!

Trims

Decorations

Materials needed:

Aluminum foil

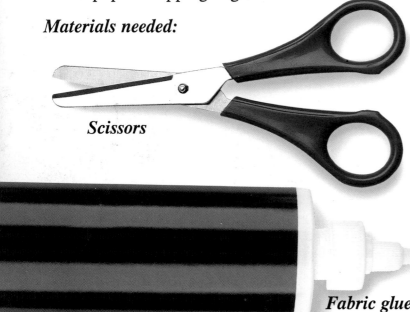

Scissors

Fabric glue

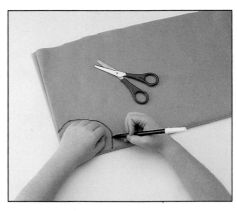

1 Fold the cloth in half. Hold it up against you to make sure it's the right length and wide enough to go from shoulder to shoulder.

2 Lay the folded cloth flat. Fold it in half again so it will be long and skinny.

3 Mark where the hole for your neck will be. Make a fist and lay it on the corner of the folded cloth. Draw a line around your fist.

Paint

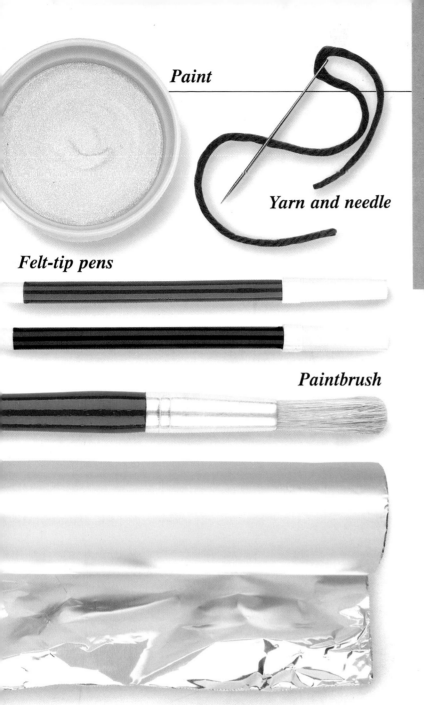

Yarn and needle

Felt-tip pens

Paintbrush

Paper shopping bags

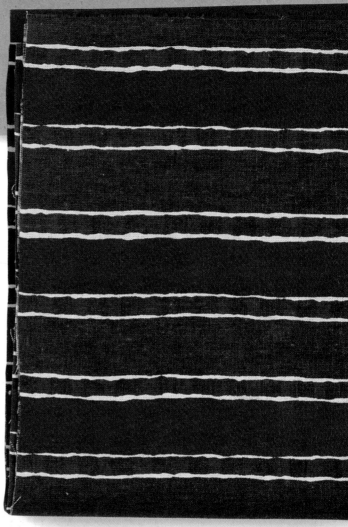

Cloth: sheet, tablecloth, felt

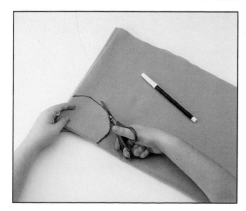

4 Cut the corner off. Cut it round (like the American Indian top on page 13) or square (like the Robin Hood top on page 12).

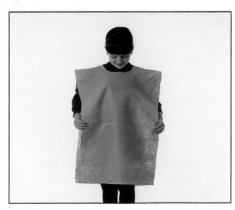

5 Unfold the top and try it on. You can trim it if it's too long. Cut the bottom straight across, cut a zigzag, or cut fringe into it!

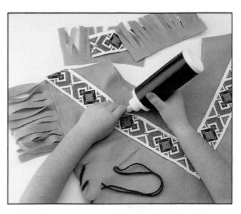

6 You can sew up the sides, leaving holes at the top for your arms. Or just hold your top closed with a belt. Add fringe and trims!

Fun Tops

◀ Here's a clown top an adult helped sew, with sleeves and a fluffy collar made from scrap cloth. The "buttons" are milk bottle tops!

▶ The dragon top is a paper bag covered with cloth scales. You could paint the scales instead of making them cloth. The belly is felt with glitter paint stripes.

Sleeves

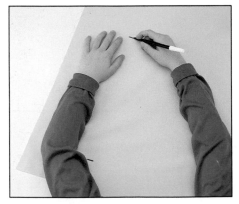

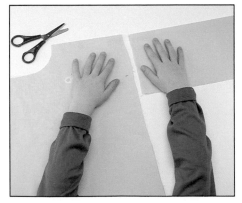

1 Here's how to add sleeves to your top. Cut two rectangles that are as long as your arm and as wide as from your elbow to your fingertips.

2 Fold each rectangle in half so they're long and skinny. Place them next to your top—put the folds next to each other.

3 Unfold the top and the rectangles. Sew or tape the pieces together.

◀ The monster's top is a paper bag painted to look like a jacket!

▶ This robot top is a paper bag with aluminum foil trim. The triangle is made of poster board. Can you see three bottle caps and fifteen noodles painted silver?

Paper Bag Top

4 Fold the top and the sleeves in half again. Sew or glue the bottom of the sleeves. Sew or glue down the sides of the top if you wish (or hold it closed with a belt).

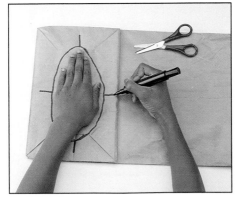

1 If you don't have cloth, use a paper grocery bag or shopping bag! Make an oval the size of your hand in the bottom of the bag. Draw four lines, as shown.

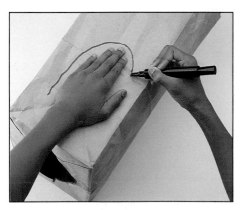

2 Cut out the oval and make small cuts where your lines are (for your head to go through). Now cut arm holes in the sides of the bag. Make them the size of your hand.

11

Topsy-Turvy

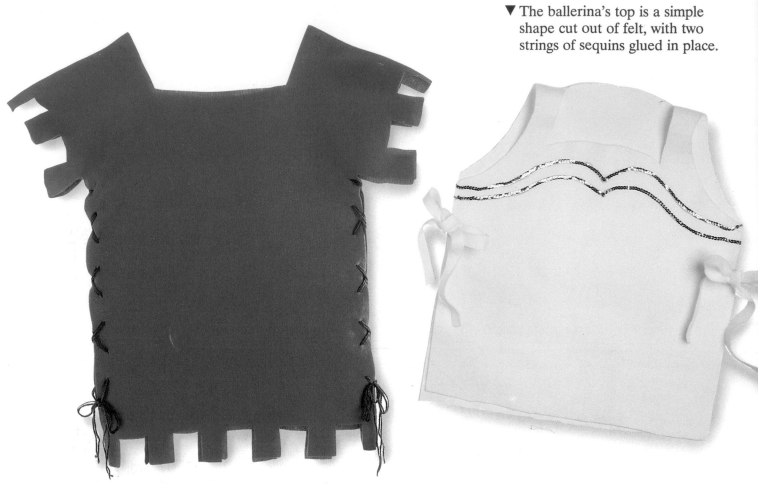

▼ The ballerina's top is a simple shape cut out of felt, with two strings of sequins glued in place.

▲ After you cut the neck hole for a Robin Hood top, unfold the cloth, cut up the sides and then out to make square sleeves.

Ballerina Top

1 Your top doesn't have to be square. You can cut it into a shape. Draw it on paper, cut it out, and try it on to make sure it will fit.

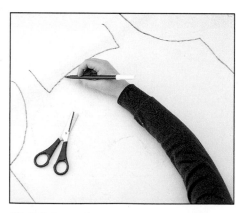

2 Make a short top following steps 1-6 on pages 8-9. Draw your shape lightly on the cloth. Then cut it out and decorate it.

3 Make four straps to pin or sew on the sides of your top, in front *and* back. Tie the back ones around your waist—*under* the front. Tie the front straps behind your back.

◀ A top with a ragged bottom is good for a pirate who's been at sea, fighting for treasure.

▼ This American Indian's top is long like a dress, sewn with yarn and trimmed with fringe.

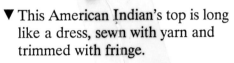

▲ The queen's gown is very long, with gold trim and beads and an old string of pearls.

13

Witch and Wizard

The best part of making costumes is putting the pieces together! Here are five finished costumes. You'll find more on other pages of this book. You don't have to copy these ideas! Use your imagination to design your own costumes.

The beard is made of fiberfill from a fabric store. It's painted gray and pinned to elastic.

The elastic is attached to the inside of the hat, and goes under the chin from ear to ear.

Hat, page 44.

The witch's hair is fiberfill; it's taped to the inside of the hat!

His wand is made of a dowel rod painted purple and a cardboard star covered with glitter.

Hat, page 44.

The wizard's wearing white gloves and holding an old glass ball flower holder.

Have an adult help you paint your face witchy green with warts!

Top, pages 8-9.

These fingernails are plastic containers florists use. They fill them with water and put cut flowers in them.

Pointy paper boots covered with silver glitter. See boots on page 35.

Boots, page 34.

14

Ghost, Robin Hood and Bee

An elastic strap holds his hat under his chin—it fits through holes cut in the sheet on either side of his head. See hats on page 44.

This ghost is a white sheet with a face cut out and red blood painted on.

He has Mylar tinsel for hair, glued onto the sheet.

The antennae are pipe cleaners and foam balls sprinkled with glitter and attached to a headband.

This bee's top is made from a pillowcase.

Aluminum foil chain.

Hat, page 45.

Weapons, page 48.

Wings, page 46.

Top, page 12.

The bee's stinger is like a cone-shaped hat (see pages 42-43). It's covered with fabric and painted. It has a gold pipe cleaner on the end. Staple black elastic to both sides of the inside of the cone. Then wear the elastic around your front.

Boots, page 34.

Skeleton feet painted on old, black socks!

Knickers

Knickers are short pants. They stop just below your knees. You can make them look three different ways at the bottom: straight across, jagged, or "gathered" like the baby doll bloomers on page 18. Knickers are worn by baseball players and football players, golfers, clowns, babies and baby dolls, princes, monsters, and pirates.

Masking tape

Materials needed:

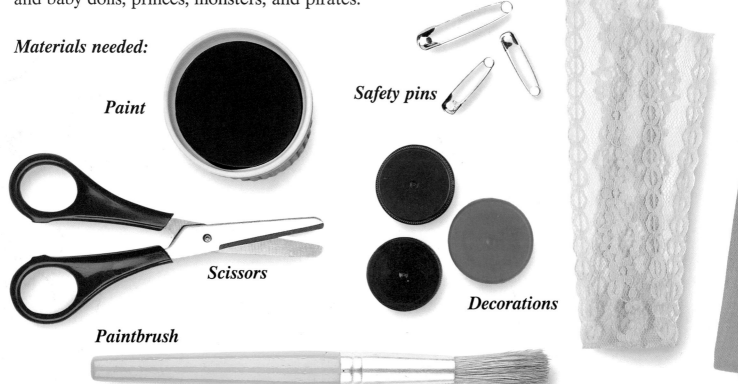

Paint

Safety pins

Scissors

Decorations

Paintbrush

Baggy Knickers

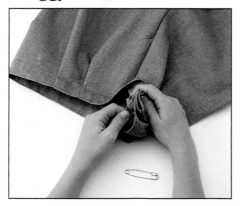

If the old pants you're using are too big, make "pleats" in the front. Pinch folds of material and pin them on the inside of the pants, like this.

Straight Knickers

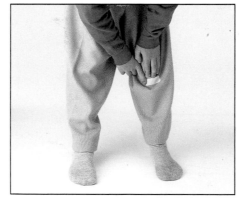

1 Put on the pants. Place your hand below your knee and measure to your fingertips. Mark the place with masking tape. Do this on both legs.

2 Take off the pants. Stuff the bottom of each pant leg up into the top of the pant legs until you get to the tape mark. Tape each leg all the way around the inside.

16

Old pants

Trims

Jagged Knickers

Measure how long your knickers should be (see step 1 on page 16). Take the pants off, cut the bottom of both pant legs off at the tape marks, and cut zigzags at the bottom.

Gathered Knickers

1 Measure how long your knickers should be (see step 1 on page 16). Cut the bottom of both pant legs off at the tape marks.

2 Measure one thumb-length up from the cut-off edge. Tape around the pant leg at that place and pull it tight to make a ruffle! Hide the tape with ribbon or lace.

17

Finished Knickers

◄ These clown pants are gathered knickers that an adult helped sew, with big polka dots cut out of felt and glued on with fabric glue.

▲ Soft colors and lace are good for baby doll bloomers.

◄ These prince knickers have fake fur for trim. Do you have an old, fuzzy rug you could cut up to make fake fur?

◀ For pirate knickers, cut fabric patches and sew them on with big stitches. Or paint them on!

▲ Ask an adult to help you use spray paint to add spooky black stripes to monster knickers.

▲ Here are knickers an athlete would wear—with knee patches!

Animal Heads

Animal heads are easy to make out of a towel and a matching washcloth. You can be any animal you want—just find a towel that's the right color.

Materials needed:

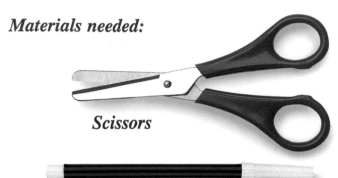

Scissors

Felt-tip pen

2 safety pins or needle and thread

Wide ribbon

Towel

Washcloth

1 Lay the towel flat. Fold one long side of the towel up. The folded part should be as wide as your hand.

2 Put the towel on, with the folded part in front. Tie the ribbon around your neck to hold it in place. Mark where the ears should be.

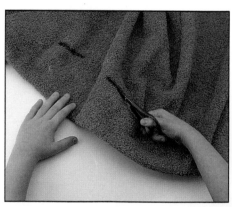

3 Take the towel off your head and make cuts where each ear mark is.

Dragon

A dragon has "spines" on his head instead of ears. Fold washcloths in half diagonally and sew or pin the folded edges to the towel. To make them stand up, glue pipe cleaners between the folded washcloth halves.

Tiger

Cut stripes out of black felt and glue them onto your tiger head. When you wear it, tuck the extra towel into the neck of your shirt.

4 Cut the washcloth in half. Fold each cut piece in half.

5 Put the fold on the left. Now fold one side to the left and one to the right to make a pointy ear shape. Do this for each ear.

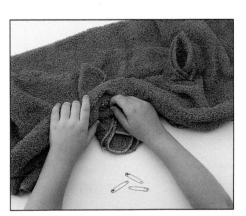

6 Fit the bottoms of the ear shapes into the cuts. Pin or sew the ears in place on the inside of the towel head.

Clown, Mermaid and Robot

Hat,
page 44.

Have an adult help
you design and paint
a clown face with
face paint.

The robot's
headpiece is a knit
cap with scouring
pads pinned on and
pipe cleaners stuck
in it!

Wrist bands made of
foil match the robot's
paper top.

Bow tie,
page 47.

Top,
page 10.

Knickers,
page 16.

Walkie-talkie,
page 47.

This mermaid's
gown is a big onion
sack from a food
market, with holes
cut for the head and
arms. She's wearing
it over a long slip
dyed green.

Hair,
page 29.

Top,
page 11.

Shoes,
pages 38-39.

Boots,
page 35.

Ballerina and Dragon

Have an adult help you design and paint a dragon face with face paint.

Head, pages 20-21.

Cut some washcloths in half diagonally, and tie them end to end to make a long tail. You can sew them or pin them to the towel hood.

The ballerina's headband is stiff paper covered with glittery stars. It's glued to elastic that was cut to fit her head.

Top, page 10.

Top, page 12.

Feet, page 37.

Get permission to wear a big, ruffly slip for a ballerina skirt.

Capes

It's fun and easy to make capes for great costumes like a king and queen, devil, vampire, witch or wizard, or superhero. You decide whether your cape should be long or short. You can make a cape out of almost anything: an old skirt, sheet, tablecloth, curtain, towel or shower curtain.

Materials needed:

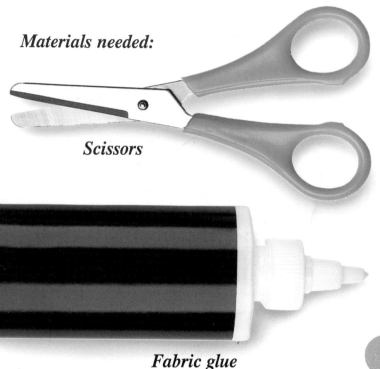

Scissors

Fabric glue

Shower curtain or other cloth

Ribbon and decorations

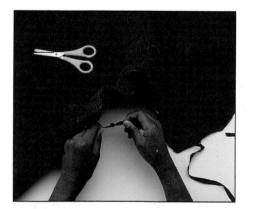

Skirt. Cut all the way up one side of a skirt. Make a hole on each side of the cut at the top. Put a piece of ribbon through each hole. Tie a knot in each ribbon on the inside of the cape.

Sheet. Cut a little hole on each side of the hemmed end of a sheet. Use a safety pin to push a long ribbon through it. Make a knot on each end of the ribbon.

Shower curtain. Get permission to use a cloth shower curtain. Put a ribbon through the holes at the top. Gather it around your shoulders and tie a knot on each end.

Queen Cape

Superhero Cape
If the skirt has a zipper, you can cut
out all the stitches and then take out
the zipper.

Wizard Cape
Add decorations to your cape:
sequins, and planets, moons, and
stars cut out of shiny fabric make this
wizard's cape special.

Armor

Fruit trays, free from a grocery store or fruit market, can become a suit of armor for a knight, or a shell for a turtle. Just add paint and a few decorations!

Materials needed:

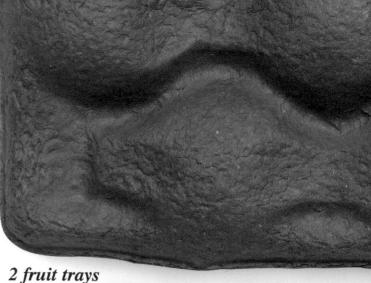

2 fruit trays

Decorations

Felt

Paint

Paintbrush

Turtle

1 Paint and decorate one fruit tray to look like the belly of a turtle and one to look like his back. It can look real or silly.

2 Make straps to go over your shoulders. Glue or tape them to the top on the inside of each painted fruit tray.

Ribbon

3 Make a belt to go all the way around your middle. Or poke holes in the sides of the fruit trays and tie a ribbon at each hole.

Turtle and Knight

A natural stick becomes a spear when you make a spearhead out of foil.

The collar is like a big felt dough-nut—with a hole in the center for your head. The edges were cut into a zigzag shape.

The knight's helmet is two stiff plastic bags folded and taped to make a cap. It's decorated with foil-covered coffee scoops, strips of foam, scouring pads, felt, and feathers.

Make a headband of felt with green sequins to match the shell.

Cut a shield out of another fruit tray and glue a stiff paper handle on the back.

This felt belt goes all the way around and ties in the back. It has shiny tinsel in the middle.

See how to make paper boot tops on page 35. These are covered with foil.

27

Hair

It's fun and easy to make hair for your costume out of yarn, nylon stockings or rope. These are just three ideas—what kind of hair will you need for *your* costume, and what will *you* make it out of?

Do you know the story of Rapunzel? She was kept in a castle tower. She let her hair grow so long that the prince could use it to climb up the tower. This Rapunzel's hair is a fat rope, pulled apart into long twists. It's glued to the inside of a cone-shaped hat (see Hats, pages 42-43).

Baby Doll Yarn Hair

American Indian Stocking Hair

Mermaid Rope Hair

Yarn Hair

1 Cut long strips of yarn—the more the better! Make them all the same length. Tie a shorter piece of yarn around the middle.

2 Glue the yarn onto a piece of poster board about 8" (20 cm) long. Cut a 14" (36 cm) piece of elastic and staple it to both ends.

3 On the top of the hair, put a thin line of glue across the middle to hold things in place. Add a bow. Cut some yarn short to make bangs.

Stocking Hair

1 Put the body part of the stockings on your head. Decide where you want the braids to start. Put rubber bands there.

2 Take the stockings off your head. Cut each leg into three long strips up to the rubber band.

3 Braid each leg by crossing the left strip over the middle, then the right strip over the middle. Tie the ends with ribbons.

Rope Hair

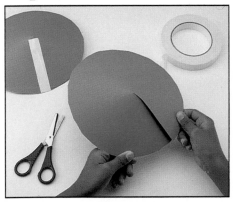  

1 Cut two paper circles the size of the top of your head. Cut into the middle of each circle. Overlap the cut edges and tape them to make two cones.

2 Cut long pieces of rope. Pull apart the different sections to make long, curly strings.

3 Make a rope sandwich! Glue the curly rope onto the top of one of the paper cones. Then glue the other cone on top of the rope. Decorate the top cone to be a hat.

Angel and Devil

A paper headband is covered with sparkly trim from a fabric store. The halo is wire garland from a craft store.

Hair, page 29.

Top, pages 8-9.

The angel's top has two layers: a white sheet and a sheer curtain. The collar is scrap cloth folded to make a ruffle.

Wings, page 46.

Slippers, page 37.

The pitchfork is wire attched to a dowel rod from a hardware store. It's covered with felt and glitter.

The devil's horns are wire attached to a headband. They're covered with felt and glitter.

Have an adult help you paint your face red and black for a real devilish look!

The tail is a stretched-out wire coat hanger covered with felt and glitter.

Boots, pages 33 and 34.

Monster and Superhero

This collar is made of paper with wine bottle corks glued on either side.

Have an adult help you paint a scary monster face with ugly scars!

This simple headband is gold fabric with a sequined star glued on. (You can make a star or buy one at a fabric or craft store.)

Top, page 11.

Cape, page 24.

Knickers, page 17.

The superhero's belt is made of paper covered with gold fabric. The red patch is sequins and the "W" is a pipe cleaner.

Shoes, pages 38-39.

The boots and wristbands are paper covered with gold fabric. The thin red stripes are painted on. See boot tops on page 35.

Cover an old pair of shoes with gold fabric or paint.

Shoes

Special shoes are the finishing touch to almost any costume. It's easy to decorate old shoes or ballet slippers. Or, make big clown shoes or animal paws out of paper lunch bags. Make your own boots out of cloth or paper. Make felt moccasins. Old socks can become bird feet. Use your imagination, and you can make any kind of feet you need!

Materials needed:

Paint

Needle and thread

Glue

Scissors

Decorations

Stapler (or tape)

Markers

Paintbrush

Old socks

Cardboard (or heavy paper)

Lunch bags and grocery bags

Devil Boots

Here's a sample of the kinds of shoes you can make and where to find directions: devil boots out of red felt and glitter (page 34), baby moccasins made with fabric and yarn (page 37), and angel shoes—ballet slippers with a cardboard piece on top (page 37).

Baby Booties

Angel Shoes

Beads and rice glued on top look like jewels!

Boots

Witch Boots

These cloth boot tops have pointy toes you can stuff with cotton or newspaper. Sew or tape elastic to go under your shoe.

Robin Hood Boots

Cloth Boot Tops

1 Wrap string around your leg where you want the top of the boot to be. Cut the piece of string that fits around your leg. Fold it in half and cut it at the fold.

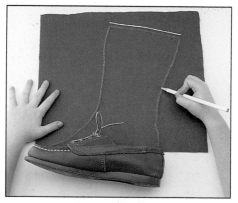

2 Lay one of your shoes sideways. Draw the side of a boot coming up from the shoe. Make the top of the boot as wide as the short pieces of string you cut.

3 Cut four of the boot shapes out of cloth. Have an adult help you sew two together for each boot. Leave the bottom open so your shoe will stick out.

Robot Boots

Covering your shoes with aluminum foil will make them match your silver boot tops.

Pirate Boots

These boot tops are made of paper grocery bags covered with black felt. The buckles are cardboard covered with gold paper.

Paper Boot Tops

1 Measure a piece of string as in step 1 on page 34. Cut another piece of string that is as long as your leg from below your knee to the top of your foot.

2 Put these two pieces of string on a grocery bag in the shape of an upside-down L. Draw the side of a boot using the strings as a guide.

3 Cut four of these paper shapes. Tape two of them together for each boot. Paint them and decorate them. Wear them over the top of your shoes.

Moccasins, Slippers and Socks

Queen (or Movie Star) Slippers

Moccasins

Here are three kinds of sock feet, from left to right: bird feet, tobi socks (with two toes instead of three), and dragon feet (shown on page 23).

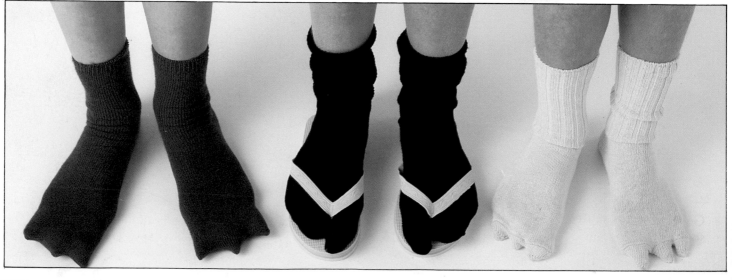

Moccasins

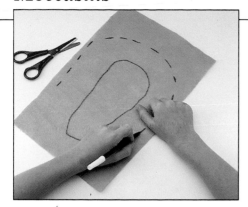

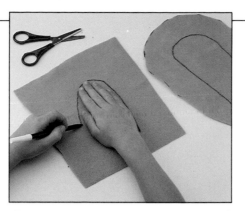

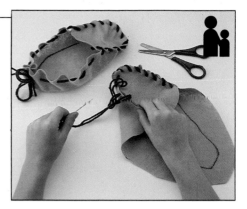

1 Stand on a piece of felt and trace around your foot. Then draw a bigger shape around your tracing using your thumb to measure. Cut out two of these.

2 Lay your hand flat and trace around it. Cut two of these shapes.

3 Have an adult help you sew the two pieces together with thick yarn. Decorate your finished moccasins with fabric trim or pompons.

Fancy Slippers

1 Lay your hand flat on a piece of cardboard. Draw an oval or triangle around your fingertips. Cut out two of these shapes.

2 Paint the cardboard shape, or cover it with felt the color of your ballet slipper. Add decorations. Make the two pieces match.

3 Roll a piece of masking tape. Stick the tape to the bottom of the cardboard piece and tape it to the top of your ballet slipper.

Sock Feet

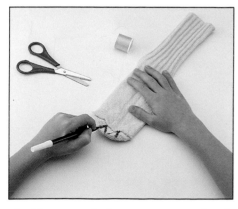

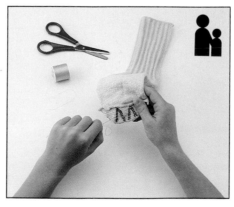

1 Get permission to use a pair of socks the color you want for the feet. Turn each sock inside out and draw two V's in the toe.

2 Have an adult help you stitch on the lines of the "V" shapes. Make lots of stitches.

3 Cut the middle of the V's. Turn the socks right-side-out and stuff newspaper scraps in the toes. Wear the sock feet over your shoes.

Big Shoes and Feet

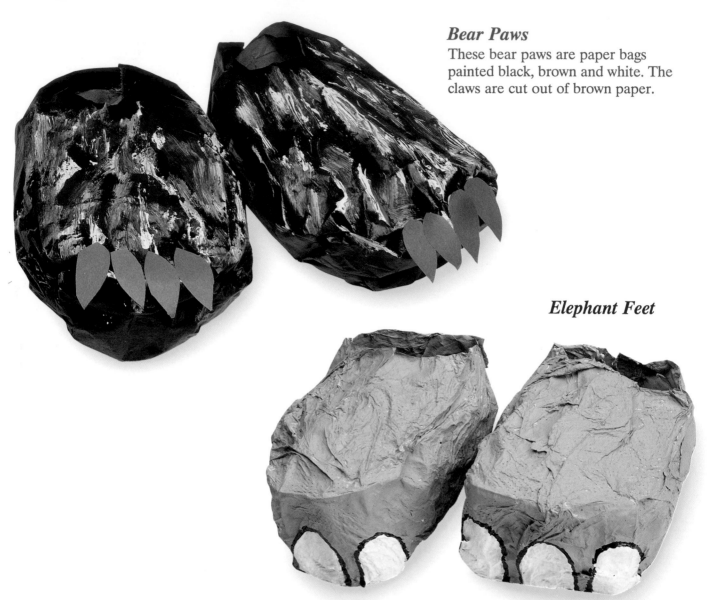

Bear Paws

These bear paws are paper bags painted black, brown and white. The claws are cut out of brown paper.

Elephant Feet

Clown Shoes

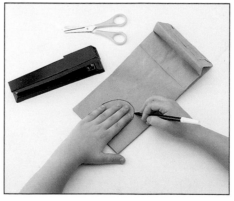

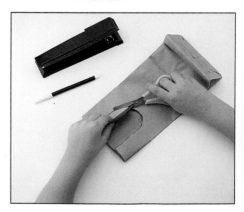

1 Make big paper shoes to wear over the top of your real shoes! For each shoe, put two lunch bags together, one inside the other.

2 Put your fingers flat at one end. Draw an oval around your fingertips.

3 Cut out the oval. Only cut through the top two layers of bags (don't cut the bottom yet).

Monster Shoes

Finished Clown Shoes

Slide your foot, with a shoe on, into the clown shoe and tape the ends around the back of your foot.

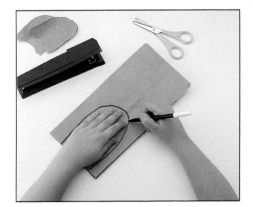

4 Turn the bags over. Lay your hand on the end of the bag that you just cut. Draw an oval around your whole hand and cut it out.

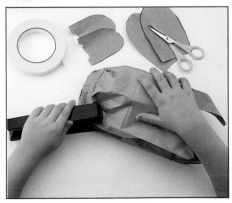

5 Pinch the toe end of the shoe into a round shape. Hold it with tape or staples.

6 Stuff the toes with newspaper. Paint and decorate. The big hole goes on the bottom and the small hole goes on the top.

Pirate and Bride

Wear a scarf or bandana on your head.

The eye patch is black felt sewn onto black elastic.

Sword, page 48.

Top, pages 8-9, and 13.

The pirate's belt is paper covered with black fabric. An old rag, folded in half and sewn or tied onto the belt, looks like a pouch for the pirate's treasures.

Knickers, page 17.

Boots, page 35.

This bride's gown, veil and sash are made of old curtains!

The veil is attached to a ribbon, tied like a headband, with fake pearl trim on the front.

This necklace is an old belt.

The sash was a ruffly *valance* (the part of curtain that goes across the top of the window).

A bouquet of silk flowers and ribbons.

Slippers, page 37.

Vampire, Indian and Queen

This vampire's cape has a collar made of thin cardboard covered with black fabric to match the cape. It's pinned to the top of the cape in back.

Have an adult help you paint your face and wear fake plastic fangs to look really scary.

A *cummerbund* is a sash worn with a tuxedo (a fancy suit). Sew it onto your top or pin it in the back.

Accessories, page 47.

Cape, page 25.

Top, pages 8-9.

The wristbands are fabric trim, sewn together with yarn.

Slippers, page 36.

The queen's belt is made of cardboard covered with fabric. You can tape it in back—it doesn't show! The fake pearls match the rest of her outfit.

This American Indian's headband is trim from a fabric store with feathers glued on. It's pinned in the back.

Hats

Hats are an important part of many great costumes. They're easy to make out of paper, paper bags or thin cardboard. You can paint them and add decorations and hair. Look through storybooks and encyclopedias for hat ideas, especially for characters like princesses, wizards, and Robin Hood. Then draw a picture of the hat you want to make, and use your sketch as a guide while you make the hat.

Masking tape

Clothespins or paper clips

Materials needed:

Glue

Felt-tip pens

Colored pencils

Paintbrush

String

Cone-shaped Hat

1 Measure your head where you want the hat to fit. Wrap a piece of string around your head. Pinch the string where the end touches it and cut it there.

2 Cut all the way up one side of a cereal box. Lay the box flat, with the printed side facing up. Cut off the flaps.

3 Roll the box into a cone shape until the big end is the size of the piece of string you cut in step 1. Hold the cone with clothespins while you measure.

Paint

*Decorations
and elastic*

Scissors

*Cereal box, heavy paper, large
sheer curtain*

Princess Hat

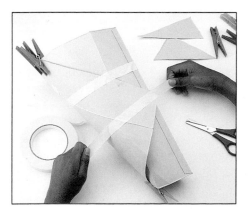

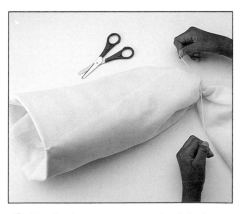

4 Cut off the bottom triangles so the hat has an even, round bottom. Wrap tape around the cone to hold it. Then remove the clips.

1 Place the hat on one corner of a big curtain. Tape the corner of the curtain to the hat. Roll the hat at an angle to the opposite corner of the curtain.

2 Push the extra curtain fabric up through the top of the hat. Tie it at the top with the piece of string you cut.

Hats

This clown hat is cone shaped (see pages 42-43). It's covered with fabric, with a feather stuck in the top. The yarn hair is glued to the inside.

The witch's hat is cone shaped (see pages 42-43) with a brim. It was painted black, allowed to dry, and then "painted" with glue to make it shiny and stiff.

The wizard's hat is cone shaped (see pages 42-43) without a brim. The stars and moons were "painted" on with glue and sprinkled with glitter.

This hat is a cap with a brim and a simple white ribbon decoration. Who would wear a hat like this?

Cap

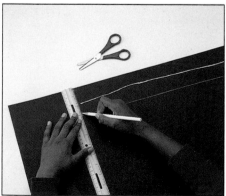

1 Use string to measure your head as in step 1 on page 42. Cut a piece of heavy paper a little longer than the string and 3″ (7½ cm) wide.

2 Tape the ends of the strip of paper together to make a ring. Set it down on another piece of paper and carefully trace around it.

3 Cut out the circle you traced in step 2. Tape it to the ring. Tape or staple a piece of elastic on the inside to go under your chin.

This blue hat is like the Robin Hood hat—two pieces of heavy paper taped together and painted. It's just a different shape. It could be worn by an army private or a flight attendant.

This Robin Hood hat was painted with green and blue-green paint, and decorated with a big button and feathers.

This princess hat (see pages 42-43) is decorated with gold trim from a fabric store. The extra roll on the bottom is made from a grocery bag, covered with fabric to match the hat.

This red hat is a cap without a brim. It's the kind of hat a hotel *bellhop* (the person who carries your suitcases to your room for you) would wear. Or, a dressed-up monkey!

Robin Hood Hat

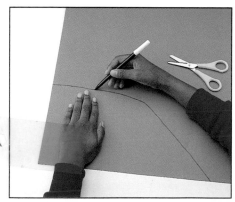

Brim. Trace around the bottom of your hat. Cut out the circle. Measure one finger-length all around. Cut out this doughnut shape and tape it to the hat.

1 Draw a roller coaster shape on heavy paper. Make the highest part a little higher than the length of your hand. Cut out two of these shapes.

2 Tape the two pieces together all around the edges. Then paint your hat and decorate it. Tape elastic on the insides to go under your chin.

Accessories

Accessories are details that make a costume more special. Accessories are easy to make and *fun*—you can really let your imagination go wild!

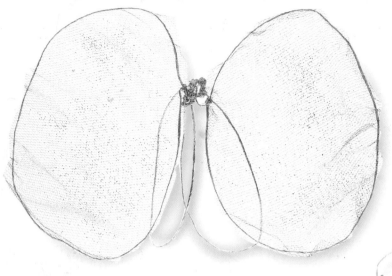

The bee's wings are made with gold wire from a craft store. Make two ovals for wings and two ovals to put your arms through. The wire is threaded through black netting that is sprinkled with glitter.

The pirate's earring is a gold curtain ring attached to elastic. The elastic goes around your whole ear! If you don't have a curtain ring, you can make one out of paper.

This angel's wings are covered with lots of white feathers. You can decorate yours however you wish!

Angel Wings

1 Put two wire coat hangers together like this and wrap masking tape around the middle to hold them.

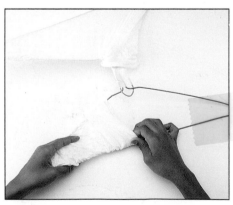

2 Cut the legs off of heavy nylon stockings. White is best for an angel. Cover each hanger with one stocking leg.

3 Tie the stocking legs together in the middle. Use a big safety pin to fasten the wings to the back of your costume.

The robot's walkie-talkie is a box wrapped with silver tape and covered with noodles that are painted silver. The antennae are black pipe cleaners.

A finished bow tie.

The queen's crown is a ring of heavy paper glued in the back. It's painted blue and has fake pearls and trim (from a craft store) glued on.

It's easy to glue paper, fabric, foil and beads onto old plastic rings to make rings for a queen, a vampire, or a bride.

The queen's scepter is a cardboard tube and a foam ball covered with gold fabric and ribbon and beads.

Bow Tie

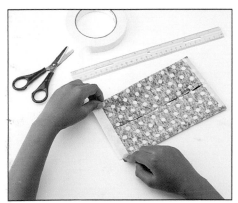

1 Cut a piece of fabric 8″ by 12″ (20 cm by 30 cm). Lay it right-side-up. Fold each end in to the middle and tape it along the sides.

2 Turn the taped fabric right-side-out. Be gentle so you don't tear the tape.

3 Cut a thin strip of fabric. Wrap it tightly around the middle. Tape it in the back. Pin it to the neck of your costume.

Weapons

Robin Hood's quiver is made of a paper grocery bag. It is cut and taped into a cylinder with a flat, round bottom taped on. The whole thing is covered with felt and yarn.

You can cut straps out of a paper bag and cover them with felt, too, and then wear the quiver on your back (see page 15). Use a string to measure on yourself how big the pieces need to be. The straps can be taped or stapled together or sewn with yarn.

The arrows are dowel rods that have paper "feathers" and felt arrowheads. The bow is a stick and some twine.

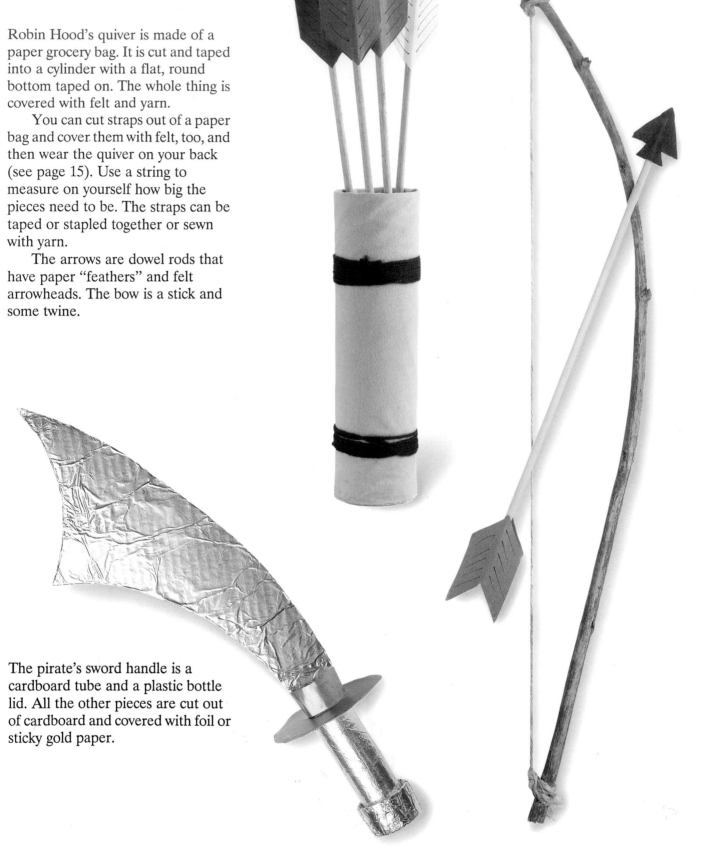

The pirate's sword handle is a cardboard tube and a plastic bottle lid. All the other pieces are cut out of cardboard and covered with foil or sticky gold paper.